A GUIDE TO THE SIMPLE LIFE

Getting the most out of life,
the simple way

Getting the most out of life, the simple way

Table of Contents

Foreword

If there's one thing that I have come to learn in the 26 years I have been on this earth, it would be to not judge a book by its cover. At two different times in my life I have had the opportunity to meet to gentlemen who, for whatever reason, took an interest in me. First, there was Mr. Tiano, who for the most random reason, decided to reach out and have a conversation with me while on vacation with his wife. While sitting at the bar of a hotel and watching the games on the television, I had a conversation I would have never expected. Through this conversation I left feeling inspired. Thinking back on the conversation, it reminds me of faith, not just from a religious standpoint, but also from a humanistic standpoint, because when he didn't have to choose to take an interest in me, he just did, and that is something I will never forget. For that, I dedicate this book to you.

Next there was Mr. Brown, who came into my center on his way home from Iraq, with a simple question: "How's everything going?" I had the opportunity to be inspired yet again. Mr. Brown and I discussed everything from politics, finance, love, books to read, you name it. I was so engulfed in the conservation we had that I was reminded of faith again. You see, for whatever reason, and because of something beyond my comprehension, these two men spoke to me. They spoke to me not just in a way where it could be considered a casual conservation, but in a way where I had no choice but to believe that someone was speaking through them, challenging me to be better than myself. I hope, through reading this book, you too can be inspired, not just to live your life in way that's considered simple, but to live life and enjoy its essence because, too often, we fail to celebrate life. The simple things get us through our day-to-day stresses. At the end of the day, no matter how hard things are, the fact that you can wake up in the morning and fight any battle again is celebration enough. Take the things you need from this book, and the things you don't want, pass them on to someone who you think it might benefit. The gift of living simple also comes with the requirement that you pass it on.

Acknowledgments

No book ever reaches the light of day without the support of many people, and A Guide to the Simple Life is no exception. I am grateful to everyone who has had an impact on my life but I would like to pay special tribute too:

Carvent L. Webb Sr. (Father)
Terether J. Webb (mother)
Ivory D. Johnson (brother)
Demetrius D. Webb (brother)
Late Ella Johnson (grandmother)
Jaime Bowman
Marcus Jenkins
Amir Holding
Joseph Norris
Kim Bradley
Cyril Jones
Curtis Rushing
Major Rick Jensen
Clanzedric Brown
Shawn Timberlake
Ryan Howell
Sal Tiano
Fayetteville State University

Timeout for the Home Team

"Maybe we have to break everything to make something better out of ourselves."
—Chuck Palahniuk

Have you ever been to that point in your life where you feel completely burnt out by the day to day activities? If the answer is yes, don't freak out; you're not alone. All too often, individuals get so caught up in the day-to-day stresses of life, whether it be school, family, work, or a combination of all three. But we put the most important part of the equation on the back burner: YOU.

Now, we can all agree that, sometimes, we make sacrifices for the greater good, but do we set aside time for ourselves to make up for that sacrifice? Making time for yourself doesn't make you a selfish or a bad person in any way, shape, form, or fashion. What it does show is that you care enough about yourself to take care of your mental, physical, emotional, and spiritual states. Remember, you're the most important element in your life. When you feel good, people around you are able to benefit from that good vibe, health, and the positivity that you put into the atmosphere.

The Fact is...

The care you give to yourself is the care you give to your loved ones. The easiest thing for someone to say, and the hardest thing to accept, is the advice to take care of you. What is shown by study after study is that stress compromises health. About 60% of Americans show signs of clinical depression, and people who have high levels of stress take more prescription medications—including those for anxiety and depression—than others in their age group. Reluctance in asking for and accepting help is a major barrier to getting the necessary respite and support. But who has the time to think about breaks when there is a diaper that needs to be changed, right? Wrong! This next section is dedicated to tips you can apply to take care of yourself.

Tips for taking care of YOU

1. Learn to air your feelings.

Don't keep them bottled up inside you. Share your sorrows and disappointments with someone you trust. Remember, expressed feelings are changed feelings.

2. Avoid comparing yourself with others by ignoring their gifts and admiring your gifts.

This kind of envy causes self-disgust. Put no one's head higher than your own.

3. Form a small group of people you can call on for emotional support.

Agree to "be there" for each other. Offer advice when it is asked for only. Listen without interrupting. Take turns talking and listening.

4. Take time to play.

Remember that play is any activity that you do just because it feels good. Remind yourself that you deserve to take time to play.

5. Don't forget to laugh, especially at yourself.

Look for the humor in things around you. Let your hair down more often. Do something silly and totally unexpected from time to time.

6. Learn to relax.

You can find books, tapes, programs, classes, instructors, and other materials to teach you how to relax. Relaxation improves the mind, helps heal your body, and feels much better than stress and tension. A rocking chair, a nice view, and soothing music are important components to finding a nurturing place. Twenty minutes of rocking in a rocking chair reduces both physical pain and anxiety; it is like giving yourself a hug. Music and sounds from nature nurture our being and lifts our spirits. Check out the website www.tuneyourbrain.com.

7. Protect your right to be human.

Don't let others put you on a pedestal. When people put you on a pedestal, they expect you to be perfect, and they feel angry when you let them down.

8. Learn to say no.

As you become comfortable saying no to unreasonable expectations, requests, or demands from others, you will discover that you have more compassion. When you do say yes to others, you will feel better about yourself and the people you're responding to.

9. Change jobs if you are miserable at work.

First, try to figure out if the job is wrong for you, or if certain people are causing you to feel miserable at work. Try paying more attention to the things you enjoy about your job, and less attention to the things that annoy you. Remember that all jobs have some unpleasant aspects.

10. Stretch your muscles.

Break a sweat. Go for a walk. Ride a bike. Park further from the door. Take the stairs. You don't need fancy clothes, club memberships, or expensive equipment to add exercise to your daily life.

11. Practice being a positive, encouraging person.

Each time you give others a word of encouragement you not only feel better, but you build up your best self.

12. Pay attention to your spiritual life.

Slow down. Practice sitting quietly. Listen to your inner voice. Spend time thinking about the things which bring peace, beauty, and serenity to your life. Find the courage to follow your own spiritual path if a traditional religion has not been helpful for you.

13. Get enough rest and sleep. Sleep at least six hours, and not more than nine hours.

If you are having difficulty sleeping, try listening to peaceful, slow music and/or do progressive relaxation just before you go to sleep.

14. Eat regularly and make healthy choices.

Skipping meals, particularly breakfast, contributes to fatigue, mood swings, and poor concentration. Healthy choices—especially with foods not high in simple sugars—maintain your blood sugars, and therefore your energy and concentration.

And Remember...

No one will take care of you better than you will take care of yourself. Make sure you take time, and continue to take time to focus on ways to enhance your body, mind, and spirit. A better you makes a better them.

Food for thought: No one will take better care of you than YOU.

Simple Ways to a Successful Relationship

"True love is like a good pair of socks: you gotta have two and they've gotta match."

Now, this is a part of the book that I think applies with any relationship. I was inspired to include this chapter mainly because it seems to be a common conversation about why there are so many unsuccessful relationships in our society. A wise man once told me that the most successful relationships are the ones you never hear about.

The Fact is...

You could read million books that tell you how to be successful in a relationship and still end up single. The fact is, everyone isn't right for everyone. Have you ever gotten into a small disagreement with your significant other, which led to a full-blown argument, and at the end of the argument, you can't even remember the original reason you started arguing? More often than not, this is a common mishap in relationships. Although we can't fully prevent this from happening, there are two important, simple things to remember:

First, no one is perfect. I say this because we tend to want perfection when we fail to truly admit our faults to our biggest critic: ourselves. There will always be disagreements, arguments, and times where our days just suck; just remember your significant other isn't the enemy.

Second, know when to turn it off. We all want that type of relationship where we can talk about any and every subject with our significant other; but we should but know our limits. A simple disagreement doesn't need to turn into a battle of wits to prove the other wrong. A healthy couple should be able to challenge the other's views, opinions, and thoughts to ensure they are thinking "critically." Just remember to be aware of the direction a conversation is going, and "know when to turn it off." It is better to change the subject than the direction of your relationship.

How to Keep it Simple…

We can all remember the things that led to us being in a relationship. Date nights, going to the movies together, cooking together, and overall just enjoying one another's presence. So why does it have to stop once you're in the relationship? The answer: It doesn't. I decided to dedicate this section of the chapter exclusively to simple things you can do to keep your relationship fresh, fun, and exciting.

Take up a hobby together. Having an open mind will always allow you try new and different things, but why try them alone? Take turns picking random hobbies that you can both do together and make the most out of it. If nothing else, you will discover things that you both like and dislike, and you'll make memories doing it.

A healthy couple is a happy couple. One of the most important things you can do to help and show support for your significant other is caring for their health, and what a better way than to workout with that person. There's a famous saying, "when you feel good, you look good," so why not look and feel good together.

Take random road trips to nowhere. Of course, with how expensive gas, is this is obviously something I wouldn't recommend all the time, but being spontaneous is sometimes good. Pick a day when you both have nothing to do, fill up the gas tank, pick a random town or city, and just "ride out." You'll force yourselves to be creative, adventurous, and more than anything, allow yourselves to have FUN doing it.

Date night. This can consist of multiple things, and there's no limit of how creative you can be. Personally, I've experienced date nights at the golf range, dinner at my favorite restaurant, cocktails together after work, at museums, poetry nights, etc. Remember: This is your relationship, so why put limits on how far it can go?

Annual vacations. Depending on your budget, financial obligations, and time off from work will depend on how often or where you can take an annual vacation. Remember, "we are focusing on keeping it simple." An annual vacation is good because it not only gives you something to look forward to with your significant other, but it also forces you to set and accomplish long-term goals together. It also informally teaches you how to save (which we will discuss later).

Group outings. What a better way to enjoy each other's company than enjoying it with close friends. Group outings with the right people can always be fun; it not only allows both of you to catch up with friends, but it sets the environment for stimulating conversations that everyone can benefit from.

Separate but equal. You never want to get so consumed in a person that you neglect your friends and family. Allow your significant other and yourself time to still hang out with friends and have time apart. You'll find yourself loving the fact that you can still have a "life," but you'll find yourself more excited to get back to your spouse to tell them about the events of the night. Remember, keep it equal; you can't want a trip to Vegas with the boys but not allow your significant other to have theirs.

Communication is the key. Whether you know it or not, if you pay close attention to the other tips to a successful relationship, they all have one common factor: communication. This is something that we have all heard before, but most people hear the word "communication" and think they have to express their emotions or feelings. Not True! Pick a television show that you both enjoy, or just a common topic that you like. Allow yourselves to talk about a variety topics; this will help the lines of communication stay open so that, if or when the serious or important topics arise, conversations are not as hard to have.

RELAX. I put this as the last tip because it can be one of the most important. For some odd reason, when people get into relationships, they tend to become more stressed and take things too seriously. Relax! Just because you are involved with someone does not mean that you have to take it so seriously.

When all else fails...

It never hurts to try again. Just remember to focus on the things that make you all happy, regardless of who likes it. Remember: It's your relationship, and not theirs.

Food for thought: Share the workload; share the reward.

A Way to Save

"If you think education is expensive, try ignorance."
–Derek Bok

D o you remember how much you spent on drinks at that party two weeks ago, or, on average, how much you spend on lunch a week? What about the $5, $10, and in some cases, $20 that you just can't even account for? We all have expenses that could be put into a miscellaneous box because we cannot truly account for it. With the nation in economic turmoil, individuals losing their life savings to falling stock prices; what better opportunity to develop simple ways to save for those rainy days.

I was told that the hardest thing about saving is actually "saving." Having the self-discipline to set a long-term objective, and sticking with that objective, seems to be a re-occurring resolution on peoples' New Year's Eve list.

But why?

We all have money that could easily go into that miscellaneous section of our budget. Sometimes it is money that we just can't account for. Why not change that box on your budget to a goal for something you want?

The Fact is...

According to CNNMoney.com: Americans are among the world's most cash-strapped people, according to the latest semi-annual survey from ACNielsen released Tuesday. Nearly a quarter (22 percent) of Americans have no money left once they've paid for their essential living expenses and spent their discretionary dollars. That puts the United States at the top of a list of 42 countries for saving futility. The United States is neck and neck with Portugal.

Saving not only creates an atmosphere of self-discipline but, in this economic atmosphere today, it's vital. According to a recent *USA TODAY* Gallup Poll, 55% of Americans say they've cut household spending as a result of lower prices in the stock market and fears about the economy. Just slightly more say they'll spend less on Christmas gifts this year than last. They're cutting back on travel for the holidays (63%), eating out at restaurants (81%), entertainment such as going to movies (72%), and household services such as housekeeping or lawn service (37%).

Make a Dollar out of 15 cents...

Saving isn't rocket science. Well, at least it shouldn't be. In this section, I provide some simple steps to introduce you into the world of savings, but it doesn't stop there. Look at a variety of different books and simple tips that can help teach you how to save money. These tips are simple things which, if truly applied to your lifestyle, can be effective.

Taking lunch vs. eating out. We all love to eat out for lunch because it can be quick and convenient. But consider this: On average, we spend an estimated $10 per day on lunch. That's an average of $50 a week, which is roughly $200 a month. Now, just image if you cut out that two weeks. You would save a $100 a month by doing something that will probably be better for you.

Make a dollar out of 15 cents. I know it may seem childish, but change can always go far. Having a change jar, where every evening you empty all your dollars and small bills, can accumulate faster than you may realize. Once that jar is full, put that into an external savings account, which is not connected to your primary account.

A penny saved is two cents with interest. The best way to save is using a high interest savings account. Research one that will be a good fit for your budget, and set it up on automatic draft. Consider this savings example: $300 a month, multiplied by 12 months, is $3,600. Now, times that $3,600 by five years, and you have $18,000. Times it by ten years, and you have $36,000. If you consider 20 years on just saving $300 a month, that's $72,000, not including interest!

Know your budget. Most individuals overspend when they don't know their budget. Sit down and look at your monthly income versus your monthly expenses. Your income should always be more than your expenses, and if you find it's not, look for ways you can reduce your expenses.

Don't settle for anything. One of the biggest mistakes people make is getting into things they don't fully understand. The government will only ensure up to $250,000 of your money, so why invest your money into something you don't truly understand, like a 401K? Sit down with the HR personnel at your job, and make them explain your 401K and the benefits it will have for you. It is YOUR MONEY. When in doubt, get a second opinion. Remember, no one will protect your money like you will, so make sure you know where it's going.

Say it once, say it twice...

Saving money doesn't have to be a dramatic life change. It's looking at the simple, everyday things we do and figuring out what we can do differently. Saving could be as easy as one less outfit a month, one less night out at the club, taking your lunch to work instead of eating out, filling up your gas tank instead of just when you run out, etc. Research! There's no point in re-inventing the wheel. Google is a god-sent tool to finding out just about anything imaginable. Make sure to set a realistic goal for yourself, and then look at what it will take to achieve that goal.

An Apple a Day Keeps the Doctor Away

"Life expectancy would grow by leaps and bounds if green vegetables smelled as good as bacon."
—Doug Larson

Now health is something we all know about. How many times have you heard from your friends, or read on various social media websites, about someone's New Year's resolution to lose weight, get in shape, or something related to being healthier? How many of those people go right back to eating and doing the same things they were doing, until the summer time approaches and they realize that extra five or ten pounds doesn't really go good with their beach outfit?

Being healthy doesn't mean that you can't occasionally indulge in your favorite ice cream, but be more conscious about how often you choose to indulge and how your body reacts to that indulgent. It's no secret that everyone is different, and with being different, our bodies genetically react to different things in different ways. We all have to know how our bodies function so that we can properly ensure our bodies aren't getting too much or too little of what we need.

The Fact is...

Rome wasn't built in a day, and neither will the idea of taking on a quick-fix diet plan. The first step in any plan is to develop the plan. Talking with your doctor and getting the facts about your body should always be the first steps into developing a realistic plan, which will not only be specifically designed and beneficial for your body, but it also makes the idea of living a healthier lifestyle tangible by starting small and gradually building. Once you have gotten the facts about your body and what healthy measures should be taken to reach your goal, the next step is to develop a timeline. I know this may sound like something tedious and easily forgotten, but constant reassurance about the progress you're making can be a great motivational tool not only for yourself, but also for friends who will notice the changes to your healthier lifestyle.

The most important step in living a healthier lifestyle is the support factor. Having people around you who will not only encourage but support your healthy lifestyle is essential to succeeding. Remember the song back in the late 90s, "Its takes two to make a thing go Right"? Well, it does! If you have a spouse, or maybe just a friend, great motivation and support factor can come from someone choosing to live a healthier lifestyle with you.

How to do it...

1. **Maintain a healthy weight.** The weight that's right for you depends on many factors, including your sex, height, age, and heredity. Excess body fat increases your chances for high blood pressure, heart disease, stroke, diabetes, some types of cancer, and other illnesses. But being too thin can increase your risk for

osteoporosis, menstrual irregularities, and other health problems. If you're constantly losing and regaining weight, a registered dietitian can help you develop sensible eating habits for successful weight management. Regular exercise is also important to maintaining a healthy weight.

2. **Reduce, don't eliminate, certain foods**. Most people eat for pleasure as well as nutrition. If your favorite foods are high in fat, salt, or sugar, the key is moderating how much of these foods you eat and how often you eat them. Identify major sources of these ingredients in your diet and make changes, if necessary. Adults who eat high-fat meats or whole-milk dairy products at every meal are probably eating too much fat. Use the Nutrition Facts panel on the food label to help balance your choices. Choosing skim or low-fat dairy products and lean cuts of meat, such as flank steak and beef round, can reduce fat intake significantly. If you love fried chicken, however, you don't have to give it up. Just eat it less often. When dining out, share it with a friend; ask for a take-home bag or a smaller portion.

3. **Remember, foods are not good or bad**. Select foods based on your total eating patterns, not whether any individual food is "good" or "bad." Don't feel guilty if you love foods such as apple pie, potato chips, candy bars, or ice cream. Eat them in moderation, and choose other foods to provide the balance and variety that are vital to good health.

Keep it Simple...

Living a healthier lifestyle can come in a variety of ways. It could be as simple as drinking one glass of red wine three times a week, cooking with olive oil instead of Crisco, or using fresh vegetables instead of canned ones. Health magazines, libraries books, and nutritionists can all be great resources for finding simple ways to incorporate things into your life that not only make you look better, but help you start to feel physically better.

5

Faith Made Easy

"The only limit to our realization of tomorrow will be our doubts of today. Let us move forward with strong and active faith."
—Franklin D. Roosevelt

Faith is word that we have all heard at some point in our lives, regardless of what religious, ethnic, or socio-economic backgrounds we come from. Faith is used when describing certain parts of religious texts, or when trying to motivate someone to persevere through a difficult time. Now I'm sure, as you started to read this section, you asked yourself, "What does faith have to do with living the simple life?" I can only answer that by saying, "Everything."

For me, faith isn't just a religious word. It's part of my core foundation. I have to have faith that the things I try and do are for the good of the people—all people. I have to have faith in knowing that although I may not see the benefits of trying to help someone today, at some point, it will be worth it. So how do you have faith when situations arise and the stresses of life start to overbear you? Look back at Chapter One and start by taking a "Time Out for the Home Team." Everything about you, for you, and too you, all starts with you. There will never be a situation that you can't figure out how to handle, because there should never be a situation that you have to feel like you have to handle alone.

The Fact is...

This section of the book isn't designed to give you any answers, tips, or suggestions on how to increase faith. That is something no book can do, regardless of what they say. Having faith is an individual, specific, task and preference. I can tell you that I have faith because I made it through some tough situations, but the truth is, I didn't always have faith in those situations. What got me through it was my faith in the people I chose to have in my life, and that they will be there to support me through the times I need them. In return, I provide the same to them.

As you read this book and start to apply some of the tips and suggestions into your everyday life, the results will not come overnight. The results may not come the first time you try them, but if you believe—if you truly believe that what you want to change can happen, and that you're motivated enough to make sure that it does happen, then that's your answer on having FAITH.

Chapter

6

Getting to the Goal

"A wise man will make more opportunities than he finds."
—Francis Bacon

G oals. It's a word that most people are familiar with, and at some point in their lifetime, is used to describe something that is desired to be accomplished. But was does a goal look like to you? It could be as simple as getting the entire task you have done for that day, or something as big as writing a book. I wanted this section to talk a little bit about the importance of setting goals and how to accomplish them.

Normally, when we hear the word "goal," many individuals think immediately about something long-term. The reality of it is YOU alone determine what type of goals you need to set for the things YOU want to accomplish, and not all of them have to be long term.

The Fact is...

Every goal doesn't and shouldn't be a long-term goal. As all humans do, we all want to make sure whatever we do has some tangible, immediate reward involved. What a better way to see the fruits of your labor than to set some short-term goals that can be easily accomplished. Short-term goals can not only reinforce discipline, but allow you to continually build upon long-term goals.

How to do the Simple Way...

Here are some tips and suggestions that you can use when setting and wanting to accomplish your goals. Remember: If there's a will, there's a way. I like to say: "As long as there's will, then there's always a way."

1. **Is it REALISTIC?** Whatever goal you want to set for yourself, make sure you're willing to do what's necessary to accomplish that goal. There's no point in setting a goal that will just fall by the wayside half way through.

2. **What's all involved?** An easy way to reinforce tip #1 is to research what's all involved. Although you may want to set a particular goal, it's important to first know everything that will be involved in accomplishing that goal.

3. **Short-term or long-term?** Regardless of the goal, there are always steps or procedures of things you have to do in order to reach that end point. Turn those steps into short-term goals. You will not only ensure that your goal doesn't fall by the wayside, but you will be able to see immediate, tangible rewards that we all look for when wanting to accomplish goals.

4. **Deadlines before bedtime.** A great tool to use when wanting to accomplish goals long-term or short is to set periodic deadlines. You will not only hold yourself accountable for ensuring your goal is accomplished, but it also allows you to re-evaluate your overall goal more frequently so that, if adjustments need to be made, they can.

And don't forget...

There's no such thing as failing when you continue to make progress. Nothing good ever came easy, and nothing great was ever great in the beginning. Whatever you set out to do, I'll be the first to tell you that it can happen. I wrote a book for heaven's sake.

Chapter 7

Final Thoughts of Thoughts

"The truth of the matter is that there's nothing you can't accomplish if: (1) You clearly decide what it is that you're absolutely committed to achieving, (2) You're willing to take massive action, (3) You notice what's working or not, and (4) You continue to change way." —Anthony Robbins

Final thoughts of my thoughts. Let's see, where should I start? I wanted to leave you with a final thought: Everything covered in this book are things that are simple enough that anyone, if they wanted, could apply in some aspect of their life. It's important that you remember one thing. What I feel is the most important thing from this book is to use what applies to YOUR life specifically. The truth is, not every suggestion, tip, or thought I put into this book will apply to your life. Take what does apply, and what doesn't, suggest to someone else.

Remember...

If no one else tells you can accomplish whatever it is that you want to accomplish, let me be the first to tell you that they are fools. The more you believe in yourself, the more people start to believe in you. Peace and blessings on your new journey in life, and in your start to living life the best way I know how: SIMPLY!

Online Resources

This section provides helpful websites you can use on your path to a simple life.

Chapter 1: Timeout for the Home Team

helpguide.org

webmd.com

menshealth.com

womenshealth.gov

menshealthnetwork.org

womenshealthmag.com

Chapter 2: Keys to a Successful Relationship

helpguide.org

askmen.com

tipsfordating.org

huffingtonpost.com

Chapter 3: A Way to Save

bankrate.com

money.cnn.com

smartaboutmoney.org

msn.com

energysavers.gov

foxbusiness.com

Chapter 4: An Apple a Day Keeps the Dr. Away

foodnetwork.com

helpguide.org

allrecipes.com

specialk.com

womenshealthmag.com

americaonthemove.org

menshealth.com

Chapter 5: Faith Made Easy

positive-thinking-principles.com

faithcrisis.com

Chapter 6: Getting to the Goal

mindtools.com

mygoals.com

Good Luck!

CPSIA information can be obtained
at www.ICGtesting.com
Printed in the USA
BVHW050023090223
658188BV00010B/125